Essay Index

FIVE TYPES

Five Types
A Book of Essays

By

Gilbert Keith Chesterton

Essay Index Reprint Series

BOOKS FOR LIBRARIES PRESS
FREEPORT, NEW YORK

Essay Index

First Published 1911
Reprinted 1969

STANDARD BOOK NUMBER:
8369-1125-3

LIBRARY OF CONGRESS CATALOG CARD NUMBER:
79-86741

PRINTED IN THE UNITED STATES OF AMERICA

CONTENTS

	PAGE
THE OPTIMISM OF BYRON . . .	1
POPE AND THE ART OF SATIRE . .	15
STEVENSON	32
ROSTAND	44
CHARLES II.	57

THE OPTIMISM OF BYRON

EVERYTHING is against our appreciating the spirit and the age of Byron. The age that has just passed from us is always like a dream when we wake in the morning, a thing incredible and centuries away. And the world of Byron seems a sad and faded world, a weird and inhuman world, where men were romantic in whiskers, ladies lived, apparently, in bowers, and the very word has the sound of a piece of stage scenery. Roses and nightingales recur in their poetry with the monotonous elegance of a wall-paper pattern. The whole is like a revel of dead men, a revel with splendid vesture and half-witted faces.

But the more shrewdly and earnestly we study the histories of men, the less ready shall we be to make use of the word 'artificial.' Nothing in the world has ever been artificial. Many customs, many dresses, many works of art are branded with artificiality because they exhibit vanity and self-consciousness: as if vanity were not a deep and elemental thing, like love and hate and the fear of death. Vanity may be found in darkling deserts, in the hermit and in the wild beasts that crawl around him. It may be good or evil, but assuredly it is not artificial: vanity is a voice out of the abyss.

THE OPTIMISM OF BYRON

The remarkable fact is, however, and it bears strongly on the present position of Byron, that when a thing is unfamiliar to us, when it is remote and the product of some other age or spirit, we think it not savage or terrible, but merely artificial. There are many instances of this : a fair one is the case of tropical plants and birds. When we see some of the monstrous and flamboyant blossoms that enrich the equatorial woods, we do not feel that they are conflagrations of nature ; silent explosions of her frightful energy. We simply find it hard to believe that they are not wax flowers grown under a glass case. When we see some of the tropic birds, with their tiny bodies attached to gigantic beaks, we do not feel that they are freaks of the fierce humour of Creation. We almost believe that they are toys out of a child's play-box, artificially carved and artificially coloured. So it is with the great convulsion of Nature which was known as Byronism. The volcano is not an extinct volcano now; it is the dead stick of a rocket. It is the remains not of a natural but of an artificial fire.

But Byron and Byronism were something immeasurably greater than anything that is represented by such a view as this: their real value and meaning are indeed little understood. The first of the mistakes about Byron lies in the fact that he is treated as a pessimist. True, he treated himself as such, but a critic can hardly have even a slight knowledge of Byron without knowing that he had the smallest amount of knowledge of himself that ever fell to the lot of an intelligent man. The real character of what is known as Byron's pessimism is better worth study than any real pessimism could ever be.

THE OPTIMISM OF BYRON

It is the standing peculiarity of this curious world of ours that almost everything in it has been extolled enthusiastically and invariably extolled to the disadvantage of everything else.

One after another almost every one of the phenomena of the universe has been declared to be alone capable of making life worth living. Books, love, business, religion, alcohol, abstract truth, private emotion, money, simplicity, mysticism, hard work, a life close to nature, a life close to Belgrave Square are every one of them passionately maintained by somebody to be so good that they redeem the evil of an otherwise indefensible world. Thus while the world is almost always condemned in summary, it is always justified, and indeed extolled, in detail after detail.

Existence has been praised and absolved

by a chorus of pessimists. The work of giving thanks to Heaven is, as it were, divided ingeniously among them. Schopenhauer is told off as a kind of librarian in the House of God, to sing the praises of the austere pleasures of the mind. Carlyle, as steward, undertakes the working department and eulogises a life of labour in the fields. Omar Khayyam is established in the cellar and swears that it is the only room in the house. Even the blackest of pessimistic artists enjoys his art. At the precise moment that he has written some shameless and terrible indictment of Creation, his one pang of joy in the achievement joins the universal chorus of gratitude, with the scent of the wild flower and the song of the bird.

Now Byron had a sensational popularity, and that popularity was, as far as

THE OPTIMISM OF BYRON

words and explanations go, founded upon his pessimism. He was adored by an overwhelming majority, almost every individual of which despised the majority of mankind. But when we come to regard the matter a little more deeply we tend in some degree to cease to believe in this popularity of the pessimist. The popularity of pure and unadulterated pessimism is an oddity; it is almost a contradiction in terms. Men would no more receive the news of the failure of existence or of the harmonious hostility of the stars with ardour or popular rejoicing than they would light bonfires for the arrival of cholera or dance a breakdown when they were condemned to be hanged. When the pessimist is popular it must always be not because he shows some things to be bad, but because he shows some things to be good. Men can only join in a chorus of praise even if it is the praise of denunciation. The man who is popular must be optimistic about something even if he is only optimistic about pessimism. And this was emphatically the case with Byron and the Byronists. Their real popularity was founded not upon the fact that they blamed everything, but upon the fact that they praised something. They heaped curses upon man, but they used man merely as a foil. The things they wished to praise by comparison were the energies of Nature. Man was to them what talk and fashion were to Carlyle, what philosophical and religious quarrels were to Omar, what the whole race after practical happiness was to Schopenhauer, the thing which must be censured in order that somebody else may be exalted. It was merely a recognition of the fact that one cannot write in white chalk except on a blackboard.

Surely it is ridiculous to maintain seriously that Byron's love of the desolate and inhuman in nature was the mark of vital scepticism and depression. When a young man can elect deliberately to walk alone in winter by the side of the shattering sea, when he takes pleasure in storms and stricken peaks, and the lawless melancholy of the older earth, we may deduce with the certainty of logic that he is very young and very happy. There is a certain darkness which we see in wine when seen in shadow; we see it again in the night that has just buried a gorgeous sunset. The wine seems black, and yet at the same time powerfully and almost impossibly red; the sky seems black, and yet at the same time to be only too dense a blend of purple and green. Such was the

darkness which lay around the Byronic
school. Darkness with them was only too
dense a purple. They would prefer the
sullen hostility of the earth because amid
all the cold and darkness their own hearts
were flaming like their own firesides.

Matters are very different with the more
modern school of doubt and lamentation.
The last movement of pessimism is perhaps expressed in Mr Aubrey Beardsley's
allegorical designs. Here we have to deal
with a pessimism which tends naturally
not towards the oldest elements of the
cosmos, but towards the last and most
fantastic fripperies of artificial life.
Byronism tended towards the desert; the
new pessimism towards the restaurant.
Byronism was a revolt against artificiality;
the new pessimism is a revolt in its favour.
The Byronic young man had an affectation
of sincerity; the decadent, going a step

deeper into the avenues of the unreal, has positively an affectation of affectation. And it is by their fopperies and their frivolities that we know that their sinister philosophy is sincere ; in their lights and garlands and ribbons we read their indwelling despair. It was so, indeed, with Byron himself ; his really bitter moments were his frivolous moments. He went on year after year calling down fire upon mankind, summoning the deluge and the destructive sea and all the ultimate energies of nature to sweep away the cities of the spawn of man. But through all this his sub-conscious mind was not that of a despairer ; on the contrary, there is something of a kind of lawless faith in thus parleying with such immense and immemorial brutalities. It was not until the time in which he wrote 'Don Juan' that he really lost his inward warmth and geniality, and a sudden shout

of hilarious laughter announced to the
world that Lord Byron had really become
a pessimist.

One of the best tests in the world of
what a poet really means is his metre.
He may be a hypocrite in his metaphysics,
but he cannot be a hypocrite in his
prosody.   And all the time that Byron's
language is of horror and emptiness, his
metre is a bounding 'pas de quatre.'   He
may arraign existence on the most deadly
charges, he may condemn it with the most
desolating verdict, but he cannot alter the
fact that on some walk in a spring morning
when all the limbs are swinging and all
the blood alive in the body, the lips may
be caught repeating:

'Oh, there's not a joy the world can
give like that it takes away,
When the glow of early youth declines
in beauty's dull decay;

THE OPTIMISM OF BYRON

'Tis not upon the cheek of youth the
blush that fades so fast,
But the tender bloom of heart is gone
ere youth itself be past.'

That automatic recitation is the answer
to the whole pessimism of Byron.

The truth is that Byron was one of a
class who may be called the unconscious
optimists, who are very often, indeed, the
most uncompromising conscious pessimists,
because the exuberance of their nature
demands for an adversary a dragon as
big as the world. But the whole of his
essential and unconscious being was spirited
and confident, and that unconscious being,
long disguised and buried under emotional
artifices, suddenly sprang into prominence
in the face of a cold, hard, political necessity. In Greece he heard the cry of
reality, and at the time that he was
dying, he began to live. He heard sud-

denly the call of that buried and sub-conscious happiness which is in all of us, and which may emerge suddenly at the sight of the grass of a meadow or the spears of the enemy.

POPE AND THE ART OF SATIRE

THE general critical theory common in this and the last century is that it was very easy for the imitators of Pope to write English poetry. The classical couplet was a thing that anyone could do. So far as that goes, one may justifiably answer by asking anyone to try. It may be easier really to have wit, than really, in the boldest and most enduring sense, to have imagination. But it is immeasurably

15

easier to pretend to have imagination than to pretend to have wit. A man may indulge in a sham rhapsody, because it may be the triumph of a rhapsody to be unintelligible. But a man cannot indulge in a sham joke, because it is the ruin of a joke to be unintelligible. A man may pretend to be a poet : he can no more pretend to be a wit than he can pretend to bring rabbits out of a hat without having learnt to be a conjuror. Therefore, it may be submitted, there was a certain discipline in the old antithetical couplet of Pope and his followers. If it did not permit of the great liberty of wisdom used by the minority of great geniuses, neither did it permit of the great liberty of folly which is used by the majority of small writers. A prophet could not be a poet in those days, perhaps, but at least a fool could not be a poet. If we take, for the sake of example, such a line as Pope's

> 'Damn with faint praise, assent with
> civil leer,'

the test is comparatively simple. A great poet would not have written such a line, perhaps. But a minor poet could not.

Supposing that a lyric poet of the new school really had to deal with such an idea as that expressed in Pope's line about Man:

> 'A being darkly wise and rudely great.'

Is it really so certain that he would go deeper into the matter than that old anti-thetical jingle goes? I venture to doubt whether he would really be any wiser or weirder or more imaginative or more profound. The one thing that he would really be, would be longer. Instead of writing

> 'A being darkly wise and rudely great,'

the contemporary poet, in his elaborately

ornamented book of verses, would produce
something like the following :—
' A creature
Of feature
More dark, more dark, more dark than
    skies,
Yea, darkly wise, yea, darkly wise :
Darkly wise as a formless fate
And if he be great
If he be great, then rudely great,
Rudely great as a plough that plies,
And darkly wise, and darkly wise.'
Have we really learnt to think more
broadly?   Or have we only learnt to spread
our thoughts thinner?   I have a dark
suspicion that a modern poet might manu-
facture an admirable lyric out of almost
every line of Pope.

There is, of course, an idea in our time
that the very antithesis of the typical line
of Pope is a mark of artificiality.   I shall

have occasion more than once to point out
that nothing in the world has ever been
artificial.   But certainly antithesis is not
artificial.   An element of paradox runs
through the whole of existence itself.   It
begins in the realm of ultimate physics
and metaphysics, in the two facts that we
cannot imagine a space that is infinite,
and that we cannot imagine a space that
is finite.   It runs through the inmost com-
plications of divinity, in that we cannot
conceive that Christ in the wilderness was
truly pure, unless we also conceive that he
desired to sin.   It runs, in the same
manner, through all the minor matters
of morals, so that we cannot imagine
courage existing except in conjunction
with fear, or magnanimity existing except
in conjunction with some temptation to
meanness.   If Pope and his followers
caught this echo of natural irrationality,

they were not any the more artificial. Their antitheses were fully in harmony with existence, which is itself a contradiction in terms.

Pope was really a great poet; he was the last great poet of civilisation. Immediately after the fall of him and his school come Burns and Byron, and the reaction towards the savage and the elemental. But to Pope civilisation was still an exciting experiment. Its perruques and ruffles were to him what feathers and bangles are to a South Sea Islander—the real romance of civilisation. And in all the forms of art which peculiarly belong to civilisation, he was supreme. In one especially he was supreme—the great and civilised art of satire. And in this we have fallen away utterly.

We have had a great revival in our time of the cult of violence and hostility.

POPE AND ART OF SATIRE

Mr Henley and his young men have an infinite number of furious epithets with which to overwhelm any one who differs from them. It is not a placid or untroubled position to be Mr Henley's enemy, though we know that it is certainly safer than to be his friend. And yet, despite all this, these people produce no satire. Political and social satire is a lost art, like pottery and stained glass. It may be worth while to make some attempt to point out a reason for this.

It may seem a singular observation to say that we are not generous enough to write great satire. This, however, is approximately a very accurate way of describing the case. To write great satire, to attack a man so that he feels the attack and half acknowledges its justice, it is necessary to have a certain intellectual magnanimity which realises the merits of

the opponent as well as his defects. This
is, indeed, only another way of putting the
simple truth that in order to attack an
army we must know not only its weak
points, but also its strong points. England in the present season and spirit fails
in satire for the same simple reason that
it fails in war : it despises the enemy. In
matters of battle and conquest we have
got firmly rooted in our minds the idea
(an idea fit for the philosophers of Bedlam)
that we can best trample on a people by
ignoring all the particular merits which
give them a chance of trampling upon us.
It has become a breach of etiquette to
praise the enemy; whereas when the enemy
is strong every honest scout ought to praise
the enemy. It is impossible to vanquish
an army without having a full account of
its strength. It is impossible to satirise
a man without having a full account of his

virtues. It is too much the custom in politics to describe a political opponent as utterly inhumane, as utterly careless of his country, as utterly cynical, which no man ever was since the beginning of the world. This kind of invective may often have a great superficial success: it may hit the mood of the moment; it may raise excitement and applause; it may impress millions. But there is one man among all those millions whom it does not impress, whom it hardly even touches; that is the man against whom it is directed. The one person for whom the whole satire has been written in vain is the man whom it is the whole object of the institution of satire to reach. He knows that such a description of him is not true. He knows that he is not utterly unpatriotic, or utterly self-seeking, or utterly barbarous and re-vengeful. He knows that he is an ordinary

man, and that he can count as many kindly
memories, as many humane instincts, as
many hours of decent work and responsi-
bility as any other ordinary man. But
behind all this he has his real weaknesses,
the real ironies of his soul: behind all these
ordinary merits lie the mean compromises,
the craven silences, the sullen vanities,
the secret brutalities, the unmanly visions
of revenge. It is to these that satire
should reach if it is to touch the man at
whom it is aimed. And to reach these
it must pass and salute a whole army of
virtues.

If we turn to the great English satirists
of the seventeenth and eighteenth centuries,
for example, we find that they had this
rough but firm grasp of the size and
strength, the value and the best points of
their adversary. Dryden, before hewing
Ahitophel in pieces, gives a splendid and

pirited account of the insane valour and
nspired cunning of the

> 'daring pilot in extremity,'

who was more untrustworthy in calm than
in storm, and

> 'Steered too near the rocks to boast
> his wit.'

The whole is, so far as it goes, a sound and
picturesque version of the great Shaftes-
bury. It would, in many ways, serve as
a very sound and picturesque account of
Lord Randolph Churchill. But here comes
in very pointedly the difference between
our modern attempts at satire and the
ancient achievement of it. The opponents
of Lord Randolph Churchill, both Liberal
and Conservative, did not satirise him
nobly and honestly, as one of those great
wits to madness near allied. They represented him as a mere puppy, a silly and
irreverent upstart whose impudence sup-

plied the lack of policy and character
Churchill had grave and even gross faults
a certain coarseness, a certain hard boyish
assertiveness, a certain lack of magnanimity
a certain peculiar patrician vulgarity. Bu
he was a much larger man than satire
depicted him, and therefore the satire
could not and did not overwhelm him
And here we have the cause of the failure
of contemporary satire, that it has no
magnanimity, that is to say, no patience
It cannot endure to be told that its
opponent has his strong points, just as
Mr Chamberlain could not endure to be
told that the Boers had a regular army.
It can be content with nothing except
persuading itself that its opponent is
utterly bad or utterly stupid—that is,
that he is what he is not and what nobody
else is. If we take any prominent politician
of the day—such, for example, as Sir

POPE AND ART OF SATIRE

William Harcourt—we shall find that
this is the point in which all party invective fails. The Tory satire at the
expense of Sir William Harcourt is always
desperately endeavouring to represent that
he is inept, that he makes a fool of himself,
that he is disagreeable and disgraceful
and untrustworthy. The defect of all this
is that we all know that it is untrue.
Everyone knows that Sir William Harcourt is not inept, but is almost the ablest
Parliamentarian now alive. Everyone
knows that he is not disagreeable or disgraceful, but a gentleman of the old school
who is on excellent social terms with his
antagonists. Everyone knows that he
is not untrustworthy, but a man of un-
impeachable honour who is much trusted.
Above all, he knows it himself, and is
therefore affected by the satire exactly
as any one of us would be if we were

accused of being black or of keeping a shop for the receiving of stolen goods. We might be angry at the libel, but not at the satire; for a man is angry at a libel because it is false, but at a satire because it is true.

Mr Henley and his young men are very fond of invective and satire : if they wish to know the reason of their failure in these things, they need only turn to the opening of Pope's superb attack upon Addison. The Henleyite's idea of satirising a man is to express a violent contempt for him, and by the heat of this to persuade others and himself that the man is contemptible. I remember reading a satiric attack on Mr Gladstone by one of the young anarchic Tories, which began by asserting that Mr Gladstone was a bad public speaker. If these people would, as I have said, go quietly and read Pope's ' Atticus,' they

would see how a great satirist approaches
a great enemy:

'Peace to all such!   But were there one
   whose fires
True genius kindles, and fair fame in-
   spires,
Blest with each talent, and each art to
   please,
And born to write, converse, and live with
   ease.
Should such a man——'

And then follows the torrent of that terrible
criticism.   Pope was not such a fool as to
try to make out that Addison was a fool.
He knew that Addison was not a fool, and
he knew that Addison knew it.   But hatred,
in Pope's case, had become so great, and, I
was almost going to say, so pure, that it
illuminated all things, as love illuminates
all things.   He said what was really wrong
with Addison; and in calm and clear and

everlasting colours he painted the picture
of the evil of the literary temperament :
'Bear like the Turk, no brother near the
  throne,
View him with scornful, yet with jealous
  eyes,
And hate for arts that caused himself to rise.

.   .   .   .   .   .

Like Cato give his little Senate laws,
And sit attentive to his own applause.
While wits and templars every sentence
  raise.
And wonder with a foolish face of praise.'
This is the kind of thing which really goes
to the mark at which it aims.   It is pene-
trated with sorrow and a kind of reverence,
and it is addressed directly to a man.
This is no mock-tournament to gain the
applause of the crowd.   It is a deadly
duel by the lonely seashore.

In current political materialism there is

everywhere the assumption that, without understanding anything of his case or his merits, we can benefit a man practically. Without understanding his case and his merits, we cannot even hurt him.

STEVENSON *

A RECENT incident has finally convinced us that Stevenson was, as we suspected, a great man. We knew from recent books that we have noticed, from the scorn of 'Ephemera Critica' and Mr George Moore, that Stevenson had the first essential qualification of a great man : that of being

* 'Robert Louis Stevenson : A Life Study in Criticism.' By H. Bellyse Baildon. Chatto & Windus.

misunderstood by his opponents. But from the book which Messrs Chatto & Windus have issued, in the same binding as Stevenson's works, 'Robert Louis Stevenson,' by Mr H. Bellyse Baildon, we learn that he has the other essential qualification, that of being misunderstood by his admirers. Mr Baildon has many interesting things to tell us about Stevenson himself, whom he knew at college. Nor are his criticisms by any means valueless. That upon the plays, especially 'Beau Austin,' is remarkably thoughtful and true. But it is a very singular fact, and goes far, as we say, to prove that Stevenson had that unfathomable quality which belongs to the great, that this admiring student of Stevenson can number and marshal all the master's work and distribute praise and blame with decision and even severity, without ever thinking for a moment of the principles of art and ethics which would have struck us as the very thing that Stevenson nearly killed himself to express.

Mr Baildon, for example, is perpetually lecturing Stevenson for his 'pessimism'; surely a strange charge against the man who has done more than any modern artist to make men ashamed of their shame of life. But he complains that, in 'The Master of Ballantrae' and 'Dr Jekyll and Mr Hyde,' Stevenson gives evil a final victory over good. Now if there was one point that Stevenson more constantly and passionately emphasised than any other it was that we must worship good for its own value and beauty, without any reference whatever to victory or failure in space and time. 'Whatever we are intended to do,' he said, 'we are not intended to succeed.' That the stars in their courses fight against virtue, that humanity is in its nature a forlorn hope, this was the very spirit that through the whole of Stevenson's work sounded a trumpet to all the brave. The story of Henry Durie is dark enough, but could any one stand beside the grave of that sodden monomaniac and not respect him ? It is strange that men should see sublime inspiration in the ruins of an old church and see none in the ruins of a man.

The author has most extraordinary ideas about Stevenson's tales of blood and spoil ; he appears to think that they prove Stevenson to have had (we use Mr Baildon's own phrase) a kind of 'homicidal mania.' 'He (Stevenson) arrives pretty much at the paradox that one can hardly be better employed than in taking life.' Mr Baildon might as well say that Dr Conan Doyle delights in committing inexplicable crimes, that Mr Clark Russell is a notorious pirate, and that Mr Wilkie Collins thought that one could hardly be better employed than in stealing moonstones and falsifying marriage registers. But Mr Baildon is scarcely alone in this error : few people have understood properly the goriness of Stevenson. Stevenson was essentially the robust schoolboy who draws skeletons and gibbets in his Latin grammar. It was not that he took pleasure in death, but that he took pleasure in life, in every muscular and emphatic action of life, even if it were an action that took the life of another.

Let us suppose that one gentleman throws a knife at another gentleman and pins him to the wall. It is scarcely necessary to remark that there are in this transaction two somewhat varying personal points of view. The point of view of the man pinned is the tragic and moral point of view, and this Stevenson showed clearly hat he understood in such stories as 'The Master of Ballantrae' and 'Weir of Herniston.' But there is another view of the matter—that in which the whole act is an abrupt and brilliant explosion of bodily vitality, like breaking a rock with a blow of a hammer, or just clearing a five-barred gate. This is the standpoint of romance, and it is the soul of 'Treasure Island' and 'The Wrecker.' It was not, indeed, that Stevenson loved men less, but that he loved clubs and pistols more. He had, in truth, in the devouring universalism of his soul, a positive love for inanimate objects such as has not been known since St Francis called the sun brother and the well sister. We feel that he was actually in love with the wooden crutch that Silver sent hurtling in the sunlight, with the box that Billy Bones left at the 'Admiral Benbow,' with the knife that Wicks drove through his own hand and the table. There is always in his work a certain clean-cut angularity which makes us remember that he was fond of cutting wood with an axe.

Stevenson's new biographer, however, cannot make any allowance for this deep-rooted poetry of mere sight and touch. He is always imputing something to Stevenson as a crime which Stevenson really professed as an object. He says of that glorious riot of horror, 'The Destroying Angel,' in 'The Dynamiter,' that it is 'highly fantastic and putting a strain on our credulity.' This is rather like describing the travels of Baron Munchausen as 'unconvincing.' The whole story of 'The Dynamiter' is a kind of humorous nightmare, and even in that story 'The Destroying Angel' is supposed to be an extravagant lie made up on the spur of the moment. It is a dream within a dream, and to accuse it of improbability is like accusing the sky of being blue. But Mr Baildon, whether from hasty reading or natural difference of taste, cannot in the least comprehend the rich and romantic irony of Stevenson's London stories. He actually says of that portentous monument of humour, Prince Florizel of Bohemia, that, 'though evidently admired by his creator, he is to me on the whole rather an irritating presence.' From this we are almost driven to believe (though desperately and against our will) that Mr Baildon thinks that Prince Florizel is to be taken seriously, as if he were a man in real life. For ourselves, Prince Florizel is almost our favourite character in fiction ; but we willingly add the proviso that if we met him in real life we should kill him.

The fact is, that the whole mass of

STEVENSON

Stevenson's spiritual and intellectual virtue
had been partly frustrated by one addi
tional virtue—that of artistic dexterity
If he had chalked up his great message or
a wall, like Walt Whitman, in large and
straggling letters, it would have startled
men like a blasphemy. But he wrote his
light-headed paradoxes in so flowing a
copy-book hand that every one supposed
they must be copy-book sentiments. He suf-
fered from his versatility, not, as is loosely
said, by not doing every department well
enough, but by doing every department
too well. As a child, cockney, pirate, or
Puritan, his disguises were so good that
most people could not see the same man
under all. It is an unjust fact that if a
man can play the fiddle, give legal opinions,
and black boots just tolerably, he is called
an Admirable Crichton, but if he does all
three thoroughly well, he is apt to be re-

garded, in the several departments as a common fiddler, a common lawyer, and a common boot-black. This is what has happened in the case of Stevenson. If ' Dr Jekyll,' ' The Master of Ballantrae,' ' The Child's Garden of Verses,' and ' Across the Plains' had been each of them one shade less perfectly done than they were, everyone would have seen that they were all parts of the same message ; but by succeeding in the proverbial miracle of being in five places at once, he has naturally convinced others that he was five different people. But the real message of Stevenson was as simple as that of Mahomet, as moral as that of Dante, as confident as that of Whitman, and as practical as that of James Watt.

The conception which unites the whole varied work of Stevenson was that romance, or the vision of the possibilities of things, was far more important than mere occurrences : that one was the soul of our life, the other the body, and that the soul was the precious thing. The germ of all his stories lies in the idea that every landscape or scrap of scenery has a soul : and that soul is a story. Standing before a stunted orchard with a broken stone wall, we may know as a mere fact that no one has been through it but an elderly female cook. But everything exists in the human soul : that orchard grows in our own brain, and there it is the shrine and theatre of some strange chance between a girl and a ragged poet and a mad farmer. Stevenson stands for the conception that ideas are the real incidents : that our fancies are our adventures. To think of a cow with wings is essentially to have met one. And this is the reason for his wide diversities of narrative : he had to make one story as rich as a ruby sunset, another as grey as a hoary monolith : for the story was the soul, or rather the meaning, of the bodily vision. It is quite inappropriate to judge 'The Teller of Tales' (as the Samoans called him) by the particular novels he wrote, as one would judge Mr George Moore by 'Esther Waters.' These novels were only the two or three of his soul's adventures that he happened to tell. But he died with a thousand stories in his heart.

ROSTAND

WHEN 'Cyrano de Bergerac' was published
it bore the subordinate title of a heroic
comedy. We have no tradition in English
literature which would justify us in calling
a comedy heroic, though there was once
a poet who called a comedy divine. By
the current modern conception, the hero
has his place in a tragedy, and the one
kind of strength which is systematically
denied to him is the strength to succeed.

44

ROSTAND

That the power of a man's spirit might possibly go to the length of turning a tragedy into a comedy is not admitted; nevertheless, almost all the primitive legends of the world are comedies, not only in the sense that they have a happy ending, but in the sense that they are based upon a certain optimistic assumption that the hero is destined to be the destroyer of the monster. Singularly enough, this modern idea of the essential disastrous character of life, when seriously considered, connects itself with a hyper-æsthetic view of tragedy and comedy which is largely due to the influence of modern France, from which the great heroic comedies of Monsieur Rostand have come. The French genius has an instinct for remedying its own evil work, and France gives always the best cure for 'Frenchiness.' The idea of comedy which is held in England by the school which

pays most attention to the technical nice
ties of art is a view which renders such
an idea as that of heroic comedy quite
impossible. The fundamental conception
in the minds of the majority of our younge
writers is that comedy is, 'par excellence,
a fragile thing. It is conceived to be a
conventional world of the most absolutely
delicate and gimcrack description. Such
stories as Mr Max Beerbohm's 'Happy
Hypocrite' are conceptions which would
vanish or fall into utter nonsense if viewed
by one single degree too seriously. But
great comedy, the comedy of Shakespeare
or Sterne, not only can be, but must be
taken seriously. There is nothing to which
a man must give himself up with more
faith and self-abandonment than to genuine
laughter. In such comedies one laughs
with the heroes and not at them. The
humour which steeps the stories of Fal-

taff and Uncle Toby is a cosmic and philosophic humour, a geniality, which goes down to the depths. It is not superficial reading, it is not even, strictly speaking, light reading. Our sympathies are as much committed to the characters as if they were the predestined victims in a Greek tragedy. The modern writer of comedies may be said to boast of the brittleness of his characters. He seems always on the eve of knocking his puppets to pieces. When John Oliver Hobbes wrote for the first time a comedy of serious emotions, she named it, with a thinly-disguised contempt for her own work, 'A Sentimental Comedy.' The ground of this conception of the artificiality of comedy is a profound pessimism. Life in the eyes of these mournful buffoons is itself an utterly tragic thing; comedy must be as hollow as a grinning mask. It is a refuge from the

world, and not even, properly speaking
a part of it. Their wit is a thin shee
of shining ice over the eternal waters o
bitterness.

'Cyrano de Bergerac' came to us as the
new decoration of an old truth, that merri
ment was one of the world's natura
flowers, and not one of its exotics. The
gigantesque levity, the flamboyant elo
quence, the Rabelaisian puns and digres
sions were seen to be once more wha
they had been in Rabelais, the mere out
bursts of a human sympathy and bravado
as old and solid as the stars. The human
spirit demanded wit as headlong and
haughty as its will. All was expressed in
the words of Cyrano at his highest moment
of happiness. 'Il me faut des géants.
An essential aspect of this question of
heroic comedy is the question of drama
in rhyme. There is nothing that affords

o easy a point of attack for the dramatic
realist as the conduct of a play in verse.
According to his canons, it is indeed
absurd to represent a number of characters
facing some terrible crisis in their lives
by capping rhymes like a party playing
bouts rimés.' In his eyes it must appear
somewhat ridiculous that two enemies
taunting each other with insupportable
insults should obligingly provide each other
with metrical spacing and neat and con-
venient rhymes. But the whole of this
view rests finally upon the fact that few
persons, if any, to-day understand what is
meant by a poetical play. It is a singular
thing that those poetical plays which are
now written in England by the most
advanced students of the drama follow
exclusively the lines of Maeterlinck, and
use verse and rhyme for the adornment
of a profoundly tragic theme. But rhyme

has a supreme appropriateness for the treatment of the higher comedy. The land of heroic comedy is, as it were, a paradise of lovers, in which it is not difficult to imagine that men could talk poetry all day long. It is far more conceivable that men's speech should flower naturally into these harmonious forms, when they are filled with the essential spirit of youth, than when they are sitting gloomily in the presence of immemorial destiny. The great error consists in supposing that poetry is an unnatural form of language. We should all like to speak poetry at the moment when we truly live, and if we do not speak it, it is because we have an impediment in our speech. It is not song that is the narrow or artificial thing, it is conversation that is a broken and stammering attempt at song. When we see men in a spiritual extravaganza, like Cyrano de Bergerac, speaking in rhyme, it is not our language disguised or distorted, but our language rounded and made whole. Rhymes answer each other as the sexes in flowers and in humanity answer each other. Men do not speak so, it is true. Even when they are inspired or in love they talk inanities. But the poetic comedy does not misrepresent the speech one half so much, as the speech misrepresents the soul. Monsieur Rostand showed even more than his usual insight when he called 'Cyrano de Bergerac' a comedy, despite the fact that, strictly speaking, it ends with disappointment and death. The essence of tragedy is a spiritual breakdown or decline, and in the great French play the spiritual sentiment mounts unceasingly until the last line. It is not the facts themselves, but our feeling about them, that makes

tragedy and comedy, and death is more
joyful in Rostand than life in Maeterlinck. The same apparent contradiction
holds good in the case of the drama of
'L'Aiglon.' Although the hero is a
weakling, the subject a fiasco, the end a
premature death and a personal disillusion-
ment, yet, in spite of this theme, which
might have been chosen for its depressing
qualities, the unconquerable pæan of the
praise of things, the ungovernable gaiety
of the poet's song swells so high that at
the end it seems to drown all the weak
voices of the characters in one crashing
chorus of great things and great men. A
multitude of mottoes might be taken from
the play to indicate and illustrate, not
only its own spirit, but much of the spirit
of modern life. When in the vision of
the field of Wagram the horrible voices
of the wounded cry out, 'Les corbeaux,

les corbeaux,' the Duke, overwhelmed
with a nightmare of hideous trivialities,
cries out, ' Où, où sont les aigles?' That
antithesis might stand alone as an in-
vocation at the beginning of the twentieth
century to the spirit of heroic comedy.
When an ex - General of Napoleon is
asked his reason for having betrayed the
Emperor he replies, 'La fatigue,' and at
that a veteran private of the Great Army
rushes forward, and crying passionately
'Et nous?' pours out a terrible description of the life lived by the common
soldier. To-day when pessimism is almost
as much a symbol of wealth and fashion
as jewels or cigars, when the pampered
heirs of the ages can sum up life in few
other words but 'la fatigue,' there might
surely come a cry from the vast mass of
common humanity from the beginning ' et
nous?' It is this potentiality for enthu-

siasm among the mass of men that makes
the function of comedy at once common
and sublime. Shakespeare's 'Much Ado
about Nothing' is a great comedy, because behind it is the whole pressure
of that love of love which is the
youth of the world, which is common
to all the young, especially to those
who swear they will die bachelors and
old maids. 'Love's Labour's Lost' is
filled with the same energy, and there
it falls even more definitely into the
scope of our subject since it is a
comedy in rhyme in which all men speak
lyrically as naturally as the birds sing in
pairing time. What the love of love is to
the Shakespearian comedies, that other and
more mysterious human passion, the love
of death, is to 'L'Aiglon.' Whether we
shall ever have in England a new tradition
of poetic comedy it is difficult at present

to say, but we shall assuredly never have it until we realise that comedy is built upon everlasting foundations in the nature of things, that it is not a thing too light to capture, but too deep to plumb. Monsieur Rostand, in his description of the Battle of Wagram, does not shrink from bringing about the Duke's ears the frightful voices of actual battle, of men torn by crows, and suffocated with blood, but when the Duke, terrified at these dreadful appeals, asks them for their final word, they all cry together, 'Vive l'Empereur!' Monsieur Rostand, perhaps, did not know that he was writing an allegory. To me that field of Wagram is the field of the modern war of literature. We hear nothing but the voices of pain; the whole is one phonograph of horror. It is right that we should hear these things, it is right that not one of them should be silenced; but these

cries of distress are not in life as they are
in modern art the only voices, they are
the voices of men, but not the voice of
man. When questioned finally and seriously as to their conception of their destiny,
men have from the beginning of time
answered in a thousand philosophies and
religions with a single voice and in a
sense most sacred and tremendous, ' Vive
l'Empereur.'

CHARLES II

THERE are a great many bonds which still connect us with Charles II., one of the idlest men of one of the idlest epochs. Among other things Charles II. represented one thing which is very rare and very satisfying; he was a real and consistent sceptic. Scepticism both in its advantages and disadvantages is greatly misunderstood in our time. There is a curious idea abroad that scepticism has some connection with such theories as materialism and atheism and secularism. This is of course a mistake; the true sceptic has nothing to do with these theories simply because they are theories. The true sceptic is as much a spiritualist as he is a materialist. He thinks that the savage dancing round an African idol stands quite as good a chance of being right as Darwin. He thinks that mysticism is every bit as rational as rationalism. He has indeed the most profound doubts as to whether St Matthew wrote his own gospel. But he has quite equally profound doubts as to whether the tree he is looking at is a tree and not a rhinoceros.

This is the real meaning of that mystery which appears so prominently in the lives of great sceptics, which appears with special prominence in the life of Charles II.

CHARLES II

I mean their constant oscillation between atheism and Roman Catholicism. Roman Catholicism is indeed a great and fixed and formidable system, but so is atheism. Atheism is indeed the most daring of all dogmas, more daring than the vision of a palpable day of judgment. For it is the assertion of a universal negative; for a man to say that there is no God in the universe is like saying that there are no insects in any of the stars.

Thus it was with that wholesome and systematic sceptic, Charles II. When he took the Sacrament according to the forms of the Roman Church in his last hour he was acting consistently as a philosopher. The wafer might not be God; similarly it might not be a wafer. To the genuine and poetical sceptic the whole world is incredible, with its bulbous mountains and its fantastic trees. The whole order of things is as outrageous as any miracle which could presume to violate it. Transubstantiation might be a dream, but if it was, it was assuredly a dream within a dream. Charles II. sought to guard himself against hell fire because he could not think hell itself more fantastic than the world as it was revealed by science. The priest crept up the staircase, the doors were closed, the few of the faithful who were present hushed themselves respectfully, and so, with every circumstance of secrecy and sanctity, with the cross uplifted and the prayers poured out, was consummated the last great act of logical unbelief.

The problem of Charles II. consists in this, that he has scarcely a moral virtue to his name, and yet he attracts us morally. We feel that some of the virtues have been dropped out in the lists

made by all the saints and sages, and
that Charles II. was pre-eminently suc-
cessful in these wild and unmentionable
virtues. The real truth of this matter
and the real relation of Charles II. to the
moral ideal is worth somewhat more ex-
haustive study.

It is a commonplace that the Restoration movement can only be understood
when considered as a reaction against
Puritanism. But it is insufficiently real-
ised that the tyranny which half frustrated
all the good work of Puritanism was of a
very peculiar kind. It was not the fire of
Puritanism, the exultation in sobriety,
the frenzy of a restraint, which passed
away; that still burns in the heart of
England, only to be quenched by the final
overwhelming sea. But it is seldom re-
membered that the Puritans were in their
day emphatically intellectual bullies, that

they relied swaggeringly on the logical necessity of Calvinism, that they bound omnipotence itself in the chains of syllogism. The Puritans fell, through the damning fact that they had a complete theory of life, through the eternal paradox that a satisfactory explanation can never satisfy. Like Brutus and the logical Romans, like the logical French Jacobins, like the logical English utilitarians, they taught the lesson that men's wants have always been right and their arguments always wrong. Reason is always a kind of brute force; those who appeal to the head rather than the heart, however pallid and polite, are necessarily men of violence. We speak of 'touching' a man's heart, but we can do nothing to his head but hit it. The tyranny of the Puritans over the bodies of men was comparatively a trifle; pikes, bullets, and conflagrations are comparatively a trifle. Their real tyranny was the tyranny of aggressive reason over the cowed and demoralised human spirit. Their brooding and raving can be forgiven, can in truth be loved and reverenced, for it is humanity on fire; hatred can be genial, madness can be homely. The Puritans fell, not because they were fanatics, but because they were rationalists.

When we consider these things, when we remember that Puritanism, which means in our day a moral and almost temperamental attitude, meant in that day a singularly arrogant logical attitude, we shall comprehend a little more the grain of good that lay in the vulgarity and triviality of the Restoration. The Restoration, of which Charles II. was a pre-eminent type, was in part a revolt of all the chaotic and unclassed parts of human nature, the parts that are left over, and will always be left over, by every rationalistic system of life. This does not merely account for the revolt of the vices and of that empty recklessness and horseplay which is sometimes more irritating than any vice. It accounts also for the return of the virtue of politeness, for that also is a nameless thing ignored by logical codes. Politeness has indeed about it something mystical; like religion, it is everywhere understood and nowhere defined. Charles is not entirely to be despised because, as the type of this movement, he let himself float upon this new tide of politeness. There was some moral and social value in his perfection in little things. He could not keep the Ten Commandments, but he kept the ten thousand commandments. His name is unconnected with any great acts of duty or sacrifice, but it is connected with a great many of those acts of magnanimous politeness, of a kind of dramatic delicacy, which lie on the dim borderland between morality and art. 'Charles II.,' said Thackeray, with unerring brevity, 'was a rascal but not a snob.' Unlike George IV. he was a gentleman, and a gentleman is a man who obeys strange statutes, not to be found in any moral text-book, and practises strange virtues nameless from the beginning of the world.

So much may be said and should be said for the Restoration, that it was the revolt of something human, if only the débris of human nature. But more cannot be said. It was emphatically a fall and not an ascent, a recoil and not an advance, a sudden weakness and not a sudden strength. That the bow of human nature was by Puritanism bent immeasurably too far, that it overstrained the soul by stretching it to the height of an almost horrible idealism, makes the collapse of the Restoration infinitely more excusable, but it does not make it any the less a collapse. Nothing can efface the essential distinction that Puritanism was one of the world's great efforts after the discovery of the true order, whereas it was the essence of the Restoration that it involved no effort at all. It is true that the Restoration was not, as has been widely assumed, the most immoral epoch of our history. Its vices cannot compare for a moment in this respect with the monstrous tragedies and almost suffocating secrecies and villainies of the Court of James I. But the dram-drinking and nose-slitting of the saturnalia of Charles II. seem at once more human and more detestable than the passions and poisons of the

Renaissance, much in the same way that a monkey appears inevitably more human and more detestable than a tiger. Compared with the Renaissance, there is something Cockney about the Restoration. Not only was it too indolent for great morality, it was too indolent even for great art. It lacked that seriousness which is needed even for the pursuit of pleasure, that discipline which is essential even to a game of lawn tennis. It would have appeared to Charles II.'s poets quite as arduous to write 'Paradise Lost' as to regain Paradise.

All old and vigorous languages abound in images and metaphors, which, though lightly and casually used, are in truth poems in themselves, and poems of a high and striking order. Perhaps no phrase is so terribly significant as the phrase 'killing time.' It is a tremendous and poetical image, the image of a kind of cosmic parricide. There is on the earth a race of revellers who do, under all their exuberance, fundamentally regard time as an enemy. Of these were Charles II. and the men of the Restoration. Whatever may have been their merits, and as we have said we think that they had merits, they can never have a place among the great representatives of the joy of life, for they belonged to those lower epicureans who kill time, as opposed to those higher epicureans who make time live.

Of a people in this temper Charles II. was the natural and rightful head. He may have been a pantomime King, but he was a King, and with all his geniality he let nobody forget it. He was not, indeed, the aimless flaneur that he has been represented. He was a patient and cunning politician, who disguised his wisdom under so perfect a mask of folly that he not only deceived his allies and opponents, but has deceived almost all the historians that have come after him. But if Charles was, as he emphatically was, the only Stuart who really achieved despotism, it was greatly due to the temper of the nation and the age. Despotism is the easiest of all governments, at any rate for the governed.

It is indeed a form of slavery, and it is the despot who is the slave. Men in a state of decadence employ professionals to fight for them, professionals to dance for them, and a professional to rule them.

Almost all the faces in the portraits of that time look, as it were, like masks put on artificially with the perruque. A strange unreality broods over the period.

CHARLES II

Distracted as we are with civic mysteries and problems, we can afford to rejoice. Our tears are less desolate than their laughter, our restraints are larger than their liberty.